The
Death
Spiral

The
Death
Spiral

Sarah
Giragosian

Black
Lawrence
Press

Black
Lawrence
Press

www.blacklawrence.com

Executive Editor: Diane Goettel
Cover Design: Zoe Norvell
Book Design: Amy Freels

Published 2020 by Black Lawrence Press.
Printed in the United States.

Contents

III. Father Absence

For Elise

I.

Emergency Procedures

Family History

In memory of my great-grandmother,
survivor of the Armenian Genocide

No god is more inscrutable than ours.
Think of how our century began: red fistfuls
of pomegranate blossoms knuckling the windows
in the early dawn, a warning missed and a call to rise.
And at the doors—the early monsters
of modernity, trained to be meticulous, expedient,
propitiated neither by suffering or the skirl of exile.
Think of your grandmother with her rabbit-beat heart
who knew something about hope's atrophied muscles
and the secrets of rubies. She scooped pomegranate seeds
into her pockets to sustain her. During the march,
god roosted in her inner ear and whispered back
such strange flashes of memory: the first clean *A*
she played on her spiked fiddle, the last goat she skinned,
the wet cord that tied her to her son, the gleam of her sister's scissors
that snipped it off, the gleam of the bayonet that killed him.
She watched her daughter's ribs peek through the skin,
and in time, realized that god is anonymous
and intimate as a nurse who can deliver pain
or take it away in the same breath.
What do we say? Our family history?
A death sentence, and yet—
you breathe. You tell me the rest.

Newtok, Alaska

Home of the Yup'ik, the earth's first climate refugees

There's not much time left,
                    the elders tell us.
                          The river slurps at the edges
of our village, and we bury our hungers in work.
          We raise homes on stilts to ballast
                    ourselves atop the ancient permafrost,
                          but it melts faster than we can build.
Sinking, we sing our children to sleep
                          in careening bedrooms, string up and dry
          strips of pike while the land pitches below our feet,
                    mush our dog teams across a crackling Jacob's ladder
                          of ice. The borders of our world are shrinking:
our kids go jigging for burbot and herring
                          from their front doors; we've seen them toeing
the drop off point like seal pups testing their power
                          and playing caribou eye in corners
where tundra's thin as teeth
                    ground down to gums
                    and sourdock sprouts from slush.

There's not much time left,
                    and outsiders tell us to start over in Anchorage,
                          city of disappearances, before we are swallowed up
by sea. We prepare to move to higher ground:
          we apply for funds, pray the government will help.
                          Exile is expensive and the elders are slipping away.
                          They say their dreams are invaded by ice-
music, sounds of cracking and whomping so loud,
    they wake with chipped teeth
                    and the taste of sea brine in their mouths.

Mammoth Resurrected

Before my birth, father was more than fossil;
      pickled in tundra, he still had his undercoat
            of grizzle, teeth, and a knee broken
                  and folded in
                    tighter than a jack knife.

When they found him as perfect
      as the day the sinkhole swallowed him,
                  they dreamed me up.

      Am I extinct?
                No. Called back,
claimed the minds that made me,
      coaxing DNA from Father's bones
           and toying with Mother's genome
to invent a new sequence for me.

Poached from another eon
      and implanted in her womb,
           swaying in time with her elephant strides,
              I grew from Mother's coos and breakneck science.
My tusk-nubs scuffed her insides,
           outscaling her womb too soon
              and stretching her belly cruelly.

And when I arrived late
      I knew that Mother,
                  who scraped her trunk against my hump
and raked her tongue through my wool,
      was mapping my flesh
           like ancestral land.
                She tested the length of me,
                    making touch memory.

Entrusted with my soft spots
            and whimpers, baby dents
and outdated ridges, she, with elephant-tact,
had no choice but to love me,
        more grandaunt than offspring,
           captor and taboo.
                I kept below the soft flaps of her breasts
           and, in the first hungers of infancy,
                I drank in the millennial air—
  choked on the seepage of benzene, mercury
        and the musk of men,
           before my mouth found her teat.

Prognosis: Releasable

As told by a raptor rehabilitator

What is belief to a bird but the compass
of the stars and skies? If the forests wilt,
as they will, and the stars and skies
are left, the raptors will
last longest. I believe this, just as I believe
the owl in its aviary will recover someday
beneath an indifferent moon.

           We are not so different:
both blinded in one eye, our pinions tied,
we are ghosts to the day, prisoners perching
in our cells by night. We know in our bones
the calculus of the wait, the rubato of the hunt,
but our recovery is slow. Still, I know
someday you will go stooping again,
and a creature will freeze in your eyeshine.
It will taste the razors of your talons,
and from its fretting and final sputter,
you'll hollow out its heart,
squeeze it in the parentheses of your beak.
Your reflexes will be a revelation to us.

           Kill with ease and be released:
this is the test of your freedom.

And there will be other tests: someday
your breeding range might be hijacked,
slashed down or burned away.
Someone might lease it to Liberty Trust,
break ground below the slippery elm,
mistake your birthright for just a nook,
phony up a house or office and call it a day.

But agile bird, as long as you sleep
here, as long as you breathe,
your every wet inhalation is a defiance
and every bone you crush in your beak
is a victory. Don't break.

          Here, in this holding place,
I will feel out cold meat
from the funk of a bucket;
I will feed it to you by hand,
whispering to you as softly as rabbit's dewlap
of your powers: ghost-swift strike,
eyes cut from onyx and blade,
your hunger for a clean kill.

Culling at the Audubon Sanctuary

Cleaning out the mouse tank,
I find a small bulge beneath wood shavings:
a dead pup, the runt, expelled from the litter.
I fear mice; I always have,
and this dead one—a little crimp
of flesh, blistered and hairless—
scampers his ghost feet up my back
and molders inside the curl of my ear.

Of course, it's natural: death, I mean,
and its quarantine; even the mother
knew that when she nudged him away.
Even he, who sipped for a day or two
from his mother's milk and power,
felt in his first moments an invisible border
she could will him over with just a touch.

Mashed together, the rest drowse
between the warm musk
of their mother and the samba beat
of seven dainty mouse hearts.
All are buoyed on a precarious lifeboat
of bodies. I toss the runt's
into the hawks' cage. The rest
will be raised to breed or be raptorkill,
but the dead one—still with me now—
twitches inside my ear,
whispering between the small bones
that even gods must wear their meat.

Poult Shares Her First Lesson

Mother was born deaf.
To her, I was a hapless forager,
peckish and scrimpy—
craggy around the eyes
even as a newborn. But she took to me
and knocked my beak away with her snood
if I picked at my quills,
spilling blood as mothers will.
She tried to satisfy my babyhood thirsts,
and I'd cast about for seeds,
whispering, *Love me, love me,*
burying my voice deep into soil
where worms drawled their O's
and fine-tuned their cravings into matter.
We'd rub our heads against her spurs
while she plucked at slugs,
mashing the fattest bits up
for her babes.

The night she killed us,
she could not hear our cries
or see us in the dark.
When we went scuttling up to her breast,
she sensed the press of predators—
pack rats, maybe. They're our size,
our gestalt, and she was protecting us.
Mother's beak never misses.
At sun up, stunned, she found us
butchered but uneaten.
A dog? A wolf?
A monster, she thought. *A massacre.*

Brothers and sisters, blind-
sided by violence, save yourselves
from heartbreak. Repeat this,
beat it into your soul if you must:
Nature is neither cruel nor moral,
but she's irrepressible
as a kink in the nervous system.

Emergency Procedures: A Lullaby

You will be your own worst terrorist,
she says, placing a curse at your cradle.
Fairy godmother, friend of Jack, she lives
to draw a crowd, induce double vision,
bazooka your little heart out
with a volley of doubts.

When the door swings open
and Terror comes skunking in,
clap for your life to let her know
you're there or start singing
that verse about the grey wolf
in the woods that eats up babes,
flanks first (you remember:
the one Mother sang those nights
she glowered you to sleep).
Terror always liked you best,
still loves to plug into the power
line of your panic and settle in,
turning every thought into a trip wire
or an open wound
you can't help but scratch.

            And you're dead
wrong if you think you don't like it—
the snakebite in your spine,
the small snips
      in your soul,
           the idea of mercy like a wet blanket.

Sheep Shearing Demonstration

Since she gets lonely in an instant
and squirms if you let her, be firm
when you force her away from the flock.

There she goes—
hooves clattering away,
she's ramming her head through iron gates;

she's nicked her eye and now—
stunned, swaying—she's yours again.
Wipe away the curve of blood under her eye.

You didn't mean to frighten her,
but you'll have to try again: clasp her head
tight now between your legs.

Stay calm when you upend her,
forcing her legs skywise. The wool will be dense
in your fingers, purled with leaves,

moist with dew. Her heart's knocking
hard against her rib cage, knitting
its rhythms into yours, and you'll need

to steel yourself, then steer the shears
through a wilderness of wool. Those wrinkles—
pull them flat so they don't catch

in the blades and remember to cover
her teats. Be sure to shave off the skirt
rife with leaves and dags; this you won't keep,

but the rest will be fleece and lanolin,
greasy, but spinnable. You'll inherit
its trace of manure, its whiff of hay

and clover. Then when you clear the cheek-
bone, keep a hand under her jaw.
Steady now. Cut the flank

close until you can see the pink
below the skin. The fleece will fall off
in waves. Her memory's sharp;

she'll remember this. But through it all,
be a pupil of her eyes. You'll see terror,
maybe trust. *This is how I will open to you.*

Secrets of the Magician's Assistant

There's more than one way
to saw a woman in half.
More than one way to vanish her.
Trust me: I've been vaporized, guillotined,
sliced into crosswise, and magicked into a rabbit
so many times I've mislaid my own limbs
(dummies of course). The Duke of Deception
now keeps an inventory of my parts:
false legs and face, jumbo thumb and chatter
teeth, rubber torso and sixth finger—
anything I could lose in a curl of smoke
or drop in the sawdust. He's a sucker
for cheap props, even got me for a steal.
But I'm a gem: who else would be his mis-
made girl, elastic lady, zig zag woman,
and still take a dagger to the head? I can pick
locks, squirrel away keys in my gums, lay still
on a bed of nails, even seem to up-
end the laws of gravity. It takes nerves
and the art of suggestion. Any nervous butcher
can cut me clean into sectors and parcel me out.
I know the trick. I know how to see the full
sum of him, and of you.

Boldface, Pants on Fire,

i'm tired of grazing in your fields of deception
i spit out spines, stingers, toxic chemistries
while you sip wheat grass from the porch.
any chameleon or anglerfish is proof:
      it's not unnatural to lie,
                but why pour your genius into it?

you are not exempt from the laws
of gravity: you've fallen too often
to forget:
      you've been the *Oops*
          in the surgery room, the opus
on the backburner   singing on blue flames.

      open your eyes: the world is not a tinderbox
and you are no match, and every day you delay
facing yourself
         to scrape your scalp against phosphorus
and burn

      but madness is no defense
          against life's hard edges:
      wall   welt   cage   organbox.

      the ecstasy of disaster's
         in the prelude   in the game
      when you are the chicken
playing possum   on a mechanical conveyer.

Wishes for Emily in the Age of Trump

Let her be the daydreamer
at the tidal pool, her fingers stroking
the splayed wings of pectoral fins,
her ears tuning in to the argot of the tongue-tied
and tongue-less, the clicking of crustaceans
and the grunts and groans of swim bladders.
Let her be as open as a starfish unfurling
to a birdless sky, an ebbing tide.
Let her make a vow to a beloved on
a switchback trail and fall asleep
with pinesap in her hair.

And let her be a collector of feathers,
a follower of snail trails, a sideways girl
listening for footfalls in the maze.
Let her be a bow, not an arrow.
A linden, not a felling ax.

When scolded for her sensitivity,
let her make art. Let her record her fevers
and her frisson in the old-growth forest.
Let her pick her own words,
slick and lustrous,
                    from the streambeds and salt marshes,
and from the mice prints in the snow:
hop   tail drag   hop   hush   and scatter.

Slave Patrols and Night Watches

"…later became modern police departments…designed to control the behaviors of minorities."
—*Victor E. Kappeler, "A Brief History of Slavery and the Origins of American Policing"*

(a found poem composed of quotes from the Slave Patrol Regulations, Rowan County, North Carolina 1825 and the Law Enforcement Oath of Honor)

Patrols shall be appointed
at least four in each Captain's district
to patrol their districts each week
in failure thereof, they shall be subject
to the penalties described by law

with glock pistols, tear gas, tasers
they will pledge their duty
to never betray the public trust

They shall have power
to inflict corporal punishment

to uphold the constitution and community
they will have the courage

They shall have power
to seize any slaves who behave
insolently or otherwise suspiciously
and hold each slave in custody

to hold themselves accountable
on their honor
they will never betray their character

Patrols shall take the following oath:
I will faithfully execute
the duties of a Patroller

a solemn pledge
a charge
the strength to withstand unethical fear

Nina

In memory of Nina Simone

A piano can be a weapon:
        cold iron, hammer, trigger—
you mastered it, blew us up
           with your love.

We're born into blood
not our own, and we need you to speak its story.
Tell us about the curse
        they place over our hearts,
           translate the wishbones we hide in our throats
                for safekeeping until the right one comes around.

              Come back tonight, sing us into being again.
Come back with your hammer and keys.
        I want to startle at the devastated world,
           its aromas and blues,
             and at you, the one,
               dancing your rage.
Enrobe me in song,
        send me back into the world,
           armed this time against its cages.

In the Event of an Emergency

Become wired like a raptor,
never flinch at artery or vein,
    broken face.
Think in terms of dart
and outline, hunt without second thought
      the heart within
           the twittering shadows, and yes:
be my imago of nerve and waiting.

Become profligate with the body
      as if it's not yours,
           as if it's not for care.
Become untethered from your mind,
      broken again.
Become half bird, half trope for
        1) ferocity
        2) fatality
        3)_____.

Become peregrine falcon:
become this beak that wounds,
this force of will and jet engine speed,
      sky diver   god of split second
   decisions   from high rise
              to pigeon strafe.

Become the body that descends
    cliffwise down the city skyline,
      200 miles per hour downward.
Go stooping for starlings,
    pouring yourself down a column
      of risk. Court breakthrough
        and wreckage,
          scatterings of wings, smashed head-
           lights.

Don't think of all the energy required
to replace a broken blood feather
from the bone up;
                    don't think of the cost
to write this when every image
is your broken face,
a flag sewn into your bones,
white on hollow bone.

Eighty Beats

Suppose that time—
not death—is the frontier
that separates us. Maybe it is less of an abyss.
You could be close—an arm's length away—
but eighty beats of a hummingbird's wings
too fast for my eyes. Look! That dash of emerald,
that dip and whirr as swift as a neuron star
spins could be you.

                Sometimes love slips
past the screen door like the neighbor's dog
in search of food. If there are cracks in this world where spirits
pass through, slow this scene—let me live in the still
when you hover in mid-air to drink the honeysuckle in.
Let me be the flower jouncing in contrapuntal swing
to your nipping bill, your otherworlding wings.

Ancraophobia

It's true: I fear the wind—
the way it deflects my will,
the way it must test what it touches:
the spring of tree limbs, the brace of a trunk,
the capacity of a thing to move
or be moved, even you and me
when we go against it. Against us
and around us, it's like a slip
of tongue that catches and spreads,
conspiring with the plants and tides,
dispersing seeds and floating voices,
toxins and empty prayers, the first whiff
of winter. Call me a coward, but I will
not be a passive chime, and I'm no merchant
chasing trade winds.

I have rules: keep an eye cocked
to every weather vane, head for cover
if a flyaway hair forecasts disaster,
and bow to prayer flags; if they should wave
in rage, let go your last tether to earth.

At night, when I feel a cold gust
off Lake Michigan or hear a warning
whistle through the throat of a beer bottle,
I get caught up—even in my dreamtime—
in its crescendo and pull,
and I know what it all means:
a sudden drop in pressure,

a hiss through the husks of a corn field, and—
further out—a deer,
restless and hunted,
with a nervous system like a barometer.
Always she high tails it to god
knows where the instant before
the storm hits.
And always I am too late.

But when love caught the crosswinds
and landed at my door, fresh in
from a flight across the ocean,
I finally understood the bright mercy of *wind-
fall*, matrix of all relation.

II.

To Kingdom Come

Origins

suppose we
were intimate
before the Bang
all of us
you and me
and the cosmos
cramped in at a point
finer than an atom

imagine the microbes and galaxies
    pinwheels and spiral arms
        fiddlehead ferns and continents
           clavicle bones and mulberry trees
               the future perfectness of today and tomorrow
            all pent up together
              every one of us bunkmates
              every one of us born
                  from life's most exuberant violence—
                our crudest selves, clouds, stews of gas
              blown to kingdom come.

The Second Moon Colony Will Not Fail,

the president promised us.
We volunteered as we always will for beauty and an exitway:
for moon,   a faraway pearl
blintering at the edge of an unfathomable sea
of stars. We volunteered for bounty
or bust up   or belief in progress,

or because the words jabbed us like a finger on a poster:

If you are a US citizen or resident alien in good health,
sign up today to voyage to the moon!

We volunteered because we were bored
or at war
or because the earth was dying
and because we would see
earthshine for the first time
from the near side of the moon.

We volunteered because we could turn
our imaginations outward or upward,
away from ourselves;
because we could scream at each other
across a soundless atmosphere,
and then make love on land where gravity is a weak thread.

We volunteered because we were reckless and had read
Robinson Crusoe through and through
and needed a way-station
for our wonder. We volunteered
despite suspecting that someday
when we have grown pale and spindly,

we will return to our lunar caves
        on a dark afternoon,
             slough off our space suits like skin,
and dream in our military bunks
        of lush warm tones
                too green to be real.

Out of Step with Songbirds and Normals,

E. kept the spiked seedpod, *Devil's Head*
in these parts, secreted away
in her pocket for power. Clogger of water-
ways, gouger of toes, it should have stayed
in Asia, but the invasives, they say,
keep spreading. E. took to it, as she took to all hanger-
ons & spiders, and like most talismans,
the secret grew inside her, even as she stopped it
from glutting another river. Left to grow,
it would become another riot
of aquatic rosettes, buoyant bladders
hogging water surfaces, plunging
water nymphs & terrapins,
sturgeons & salamanders, in-
to one more weaponized world.
Unchecked by insects, it would mean
another millpond flooded with millions
of pods, their silhouettes shaped like bats,
their ears real, flesh-cutting spines
that would snarl & still goose feathers.
E., ward of the seedpod, outsider
still, grew more & more beautiful,
grew into the guardian of an entire world.

Night Shift

Death interrupts me.
I know her *shreee-shreee*
means it's too late to run.
Half-assailant, half-angel,
she is owl, white as bone
with wings that surround me
like a royal robe. Up and out:
a vector of leaving off.
Up: a syllable, a talon point
finding the veins in my nape,
the seams of me ripping,
the heat rising, a weave of feathers.
A flood, a love I can't name,
passes all around me, and for a split
second, I am upside down,
caught up in her down and wind-
scoured by her speed. And when
she beds down above the forest,
I am already dead. No seams up here.
The sky is hers and mine.
I never ebb. I enter her dreams.
Her body takes me travelling.

Bearings

"[Paleolithic] people were sealing their own or others' hands into the walls...the hands reached into the spiritual realm behind the membrane of the rock, though in this case paint acted as a solvent that dissolved the rock."
—D. Lewis-Williams and J. Clottes in *The Shamans of Prehistory*

Between deathwatch and firewatch,
I dream in fits of our slog across the valley.

I dream of winter's claw inside my belly,
and hyena-starvelings, mad with hunger,

who found Pabas alone. I dream of Ammama with spear,
and me, too late. I dream of Pabas scraping his nails

into shale and schist, crying out for help.
I dream of his muscle and hide all out and red,

and the death pack, playing with their kill.
I dream of Bear, unbidden, a red-tipped blaze,

who flared up on boulders, teeth bared,
and drove them away.

                    *

Pabas pulls me up from the undertow,
rouses me from sleep back to the cave.

The hyenas, he says, are braying, calling to him
from afterworld. *Rest, Pabas*, I say,

but he is a thrashing turtle
on a bone hook, speaking from otherwhere

of his apartness. I point to hearth, to kin,
but he sees his killers in smoke-blear and fever.

His lifeblood seeps and seeps,
and Ammama digs out teeth from his raked chest

that pierce the cave-gloom like stars.
I make a dressing from his pelt,

and sing of sun at day's end.
I sing with throat stone-dry.

            *

All night, Ammama scours Pabas' chest with oil.
She gives him orts of reindeer, root

of yarrow, coos of affection. When he rasps,
she warms snowmelt and mugwort,

then siphons it down his throat.
When he shivers, she wraps him in mammoth hide.

When it's time, she makes a paste
of red ochre and binder from hard cave water,

and when his breath slows, she stencils his hand
into stone, so that what has been—

body and spirit—is knitted into what will be.
To you and me, cave wall is thick, she says,

*but Pabas' hand dissolves all walls, and he will travel
to afterworld. Bear will lead him.*

She knows how to coax Ibex
and Bison from rock face and shadow,

and now, finger daubed in paint,
she rubs Bear into being. First, arch of back and rump,

next hind and forelimbs, belly and face,
snout dug into a crevice. For his coat, she blows

russet paint through hollow bone,
then makes grizzle with wads of dry moss.

In last firelight, Bear slinks into a crook of wall.
He rustles back into my dreams.

                          *

Later that night, before Ammama and Bear showed Pabas
the way back, I bathed his joints in mud,

loosening them for his passage ahead. By sunbreak,
he slipped through; and I knew

the stone of his body and the stone of earth were one.
We made music of our tears and went on after burial.

Addendum: Cave Speaks

comb through me carefully enough
and you will come across the secrets
i hold in my throat: the root
of patience, the worked flints
and remains of pits dug out
for ovens, the earliest cravings
for meaning, and the blood relationship
between mammal and stone,
heartache and animal.
believe me: stone does not equivocate.

how could i forget an age
before hands   before cavefish went blind
before bedtime stories and bed-
streams   before echo   before rainfall
i was there
the hot center below

Dark Energy

Pert Experimental Question Number One

So if it's true &
   the book of the universe
      is getting its spine yanked off   &
         if the pages of tree pulp
            where we place our facts are   stretching
               apart   wider and wider,   tree ring after tree ring &
            if there is no teasing apart the   real
          from the unknown,
             vast bulk of the universe,
               then what in heaven and hell
                  are   we   waiting for?

Dirty Energy

Pert Experimental Question Number Two

What sort of people,
goose stepping into their zero hour,
would buy into another
                              politics & philosophy
                  that omit soil,
the very matter of
                        city & love?

Terlingua, TX Haibun

In the ghost town, a way station until E.'s wedding, you keep your vow to a dry-tongued silence. You heed every rustle of snakeweed and honeyed blessing, stay clear of cowboy eyes and jackknives, freshly sharpened. If secrecy is the heirloom of the desert, I will plant ours in the mouth of a horned lizard. She'll puff out in the sun or weep tears of blood, making herself difficult to swallow. You'll drink in the mountains, the Chisos to the east, and the side show below the patio: a pair of baby heads growing toadstool red and a couple throwing shade with their glances, desert-toughened from the inside out. Later, we'll pick our way through the basins, touring despite all there is to watch out for: crumbling adobe walls, toxic ore, the parts of rusted-out Fords, their fenders and sheet metal left out like offerings to some burnt out god above. A stray dogo circles and circles the back lot, pisses steam, and wanders free. Tethered, a toddler tries and tries to pluck the reddest rocks, the killing ones, against the tug of a fraying leash. A woman pulls a drag on the other end. *Back in the good days*, the bar man says (meaning the war), *our miners fished out cinnabar by the barrows from the desert. And Lord, what a time. Mercury ran in their veins. The government money flowed in like a salve.* Your eyes tell me that the smell of him is under your nose: car grease and dinosaur climate, the underwing of a turkey vulture. They say not far from here, just south of the border, women go missing. Deep below us, I can feel the earth absorbing Mariposa Mine molecule by molecule, easing the metals back. We keep our hands pinned

down. Our eyes thump
against each other like moths
keeping under wraps.

Denning's Point

Beacon, NY

Between rushes and prickle bushes,
seedpods like horned knots stud
the point. They're alien, invasives
from Asia, teeming and knife-
sharp, but Devil's Heads to the kids
who fling them into the Hudson River
or at each other until the spines, spiked
like caltrops, cut the skin.

> *Come here,*
a mother yells, swiping
at her daughter's calves, veined
with silt and blooming blood, then sends
her back to the river.

> *Let the wound breathe.*

A dozen plastic kayaks, buttercup-bright,
cast off the banks, heading for the heart
of the river. Once this estuary ran
thick with ghosts, poisoned sea-
robins and bloated flounders;
their upturned bellies winked
a lavender blush against a scorching god.

> And some say PCB oils still leach
from bedrock below the Hudson Falls
Plant, but locals claim the river's coming back.

> Some spirits never left.

When I stray from the trail,
I feel them, wounded but steadfast,
not to be uprooted again.

Their blessed ground, sunk
under concrete and brickworks,
once stretched all the way
to the Housatonic.

Bounce the spirits' names on your tongue:
Wappinger and Wiccapee, and let others come
if they will: Washington, Hamilton,
Hudson and Denning. Tycoons and Presidents,
Chieftains and foresters.
                    Can there ever be a calculus
for the crimes of empire?
And by whose reckoning?

          Let the wound breathe.

Tally the points of contact
made here, this place of revolution
and sewage, of hard labor where immigrants,
black and blue, mined oceans
of clay from glacial till and outwash
rich but finite. Tally the invasives
choking the river, thriving—as they do—
on disturbed ground with decades to go
until they decay.

          The ruins remain—
bricks snagging the trail, each signed
DPBW: intaglio of industry
or disaster, depending on who you ask.

But don't mistake me: it's not just
the brickworks eroding back
to earth. When Denning's men
stumbled upon the Indian burial grounds,
the foremen would not be delayed
and ordered the corpses into the kiln
with the kaolin and shale. They left the clay

and bones to drone in the fires
and sold them off for a killing
after the Great Fire.

And upon their stolen island,
Manhattanites re-built their mean streets
from the stolen bones
of the Wiccapee, the Shenandoah.

       Browse the classifieds:
brownstones, you'll see, will cost
an arm and leg beyond your reckoning.

River Road

Rio Grande

The desert greets us, outliers
bound for the river, with spines
and sotol, and a man with a cracked face
thumping along in the back of a pickup.
Every station's a dead end,
drawling country or proclaiming the Good News
with venom. America's in the front seat
with us, ever emphatic, a little wild-eyed,
and we tune him out with our familiar argot:
Coucou, love? Ca va?
                Bon, a bit tired.
You crack our windows halfway.
On the highway, we're on the lookout
for America's vanishing point; we've come
for the border, not for the barbeque, not for the locals
with grit caked into their Levi's,
not for their locked up ranches with names
like La Esperanza and Wayward Seed Farm,
not even for the sun, annihilator above.

We're on the lookout for the border,
not for the border patrol, where we're stopped
and questioned, where we halt our affection
and you fish out your green card.
America's rehearsing his blunt sand trap
quiz: *You're married? You're French?*
He sinks deeper. *Married*'s a spit in the eye,
French is two.

They say that cattle will stretch their heads
              through barbed wire if they like
                          what they see on the other side.

At the sight of water, the overused river
that tongues Mexico, we ditch our shorts and leap in,
our hands little fish around our hips.
And wild horses at either bank are sipping in time,
slipping in and out, crossing the spit at a whim.
Here, it goes without saying, horse lays down
with *caballo*, and we listen, our bodies rhyming,
at the cusp of understanding.
The river speaks the same otherwise.

The Fourth Anniversary

Bad luck to seed the wedding gown
hydrangea before the green card
arrives, we thought, though we were wedded
four years ago, the first time the law
let us. Last night, lightheaded
with wine, our guests spoke of freedom:
how we have it, how others do not,
how lucky to be in this country!
He passed the bird, she passed the salt,
both needing a little bloodshed for paradise,
and in my dreams that night, ICE
burst onto the scene, cattle wagons in tow,
to plaster eviction notices everywhere:
on our doors, our nicked tables,
the sheets on our bed. Snouting the air,
they found us in bed, voided her green card,
drummed Yankee Doodle do or die
into our heads. When we wouldn't sing
along, they deemed us all security risks.
When I woke to the twilight's last gleaming,
I planted my heart under the wedding gown,
the tread of my blackest boots
tamping down the earth.

The Death Spiral

The [American bald eagles'] . . . cartwheel display or death spiral . . . is chief among their spectacular courtship rituals . . . The two soar up to high altitude, lock talons, and tumble and cartwheel toward Earth. They let go before reaching the ground—except when they don't.
—Patricia Edmonds, *National Geographic*

Suppose that to marry is to defy death
    talon to talon,
        to promise to learn together the art
           of freefalling as mutual deference.

Suppose the law decrees your desire
    unruly, your bodies sylphs
      or outlaws, but call it sacrifice
        or symbiosis, you will be one.

Suppose that—
    despite cartwheeling down
        an updraft of air to the upsurging details
below: (skyscraper,
               factory, tree, tree
car, car, car—),
              you study only the pale
        cream moons of her eyes
             stricken below their hood,
      cincture of her wingspan, wind-riffled,
& the muscly clutch
      of her tendons sounding blood.

Suppose that just before pavement
    hits your skulls, there is the ripening
of a moment, a toehold in grace,
      when you both untangle,

roll out of your death dance,
     & fall upwards, in thrall of sky,
         backdrop of brambles, scrim of tree-
            tops. Suppose catastrophe's averted

for the moment, but always you'll be
         on the cusp of it. She, the thermals,
& the warming skies are all
     you can be sure of. You'll preen
on the moon if you must.

Another Fierce, Exquisite Species

for jil

If we can decode their buzz and wag,
their bee ballet, that means roughly,
                    Nectar this way!
and they, another poisoned species,
pollinate a billion dollar industry,
can the semis that haul hives
from New York orchards
                    to crop farms in California
feel in their engines and axles
the whirr of a billion wings,
a cargo frantic for blossoms?
                    Honey,
put your ear to the semi's sweetest
parts, listen: that swarm and flurry
inside there's too, too precious.
                    Save the bees
and be saved, but some creatures
are too pricey to be free.
                    And the sheriff of our county
swears into the camera that the season
of hive heists has come.
                    Keep a close eye
on your hives, says the farmer,
who lost his to thieves.
The cops caught them
thirty miles south on a family farm.
We need the bees to feed our family,
the couple tells the judge.
They'll cool off until Friday.
The land of milk and honey can wait.

America: Revenge Poem #4

Make it fun! scream the billboards,
the ammo shop signs, the babes
flouncing their assets in fringe
bikinis. Who doesn't love God's country—

its condos and tennis courts, its acid rain,
its public shakedowns for total devotion?
Who doesn't love the rhetorical skills
of a cheese grater? Or the persecuting spirit

of Cotton Mather? Who doesn't love
a good patriot, venal and dewy-eyed, with a habit
of making fun an injunction? Who doesn't love
to be hoodwinked, then flopped into a plastic

baggie world of gimmickry and tap water
spiked with methanol? Who doesn't love a blade
at the back, a blindfold over the eyes, and an open
grave ten paces away? Who doesn't love

a land that's made into a stage for a tyrant's
psychosis, a president who leaves democracy
on the cutting room floor, and commits
only to mannequins and his own demons?

Who doesn't love an epitaph that reads,
Our beloved drank the Kool Aid and blamed
the underclass for her ills. She bought the lie
that the litter on the highway was a scene of crime

while the rest of us mined the earth dry.
What is redemption? If it is to be in charge,
then charter a sailor and jet skis
and private tour your way around my mind

too gaslighted by Sparkle the Racist, Boo Boo
the Homophobe, and Frisky the Sexist
to be any good to you now. *But I feel triggered*,
says the frat boy in the front row, fun as a sarcoma.

Thirst in the Chihuahuan Desert

"Such are the hidden uses of adversity."
—Aldo Leopold, *Sand County Almanac*

Woozy from the sun, we go Thelma & Louise-ing
our way across the desert, kingdom of desert spoon
and shin dagger, cowboy hips bulked up with shotguns,
and longhorns like brides of dust, waiting for a kiss of rain.
We catch coyote on her daily beat
tallying the days without. She's not quite hamstrung
with hunger yet; she'll eat mesquite beans
if it comes to that, but she'd rather flush jackrabbits
out of snakeweed. *Move on, gringos*, she says,
and we do; we're not hardwired for hardship
the way she is—we weren't born under this hot dead
pan sky. You anchor me, fingertip at my knee.
We're not prudent like the barrel cactus, built
to store water in drought, or patient like the century plant
that waits fifteen years to bloom. We're fiery
like the ocotillo in spring that rises from twisted spires
to advertise clusters of exuberant red blooms,
vivid slips of tongue, to hummingbirds and carpenter bees.
I try out the language of wooing in this parched land.
Vertical means *sun*. Beeline means *let's go!*
Red means *Drink, traveler*; drink this sudden lushness.

Why I Say It

When I talk of love, I mean the rapt owls,
shy gods, and all the cats in the high grass
that cannot take their eyes off you.
And there are other spies: clement seals,
for example, with their heads plucked up
as if by strings who show up near our rock
to sun on the cold days that take root
in the spine. They come to bray out
the language of spring to you.

When I talk of love, I mean the rogue
planets, the algae as intricate
as capillaries that drift along,
hoping to collide with you and stick,
accident of gravity and kinetics.
Desire is physics.
I mean the ocean on Jupiter's ice-
moon that does not know how or why
it should muscle you back to shore.
It wants you for keeps.

When I talk of love, I mean the way
you chat up your spider plants
and begonias each morning
and play shadow puppets with the cat
when she's listless. I mean the way
Venus looked that night in the desert,
a lush brilliance. *Beautiful*,
I said for the billionth time,
as if you needed to hear it.

Lover as the Third Kingdom

You are a world unto yourself,
not even sun-dependent.
I savor your base notes of snakeskin
and charred pine and seek you out
in cemeteries, even root through the rot-
softening ground. You seem to spring
up overnight, a sudden toadstool
under the dominion of moon.
I love the long, long roots of you
stringing forth below my feet,
acres of syntax elusive and ancient,
threaded to tree growth, tasting
of smoke and bitter almond.
What dreams, fed by moonshine and dying
elm, do you dream below your cap?
What sorts of visions engender gills,
fleshy trumpets, monkey heads, and oyster
shelves stacked on trees with fish-
iridescent moss? What dreams make
you emulate the rarest azure sky,
inspire you to decompose
the dead, then conspire with rootlets
in the deep shade, clearing space for us?

III.

Father Absence

Father Absence,

             how many times have the worms,
browsing through leaves and broken-down bones,
                              ingested my cells?
             I am alive, but so close to humus,
                    easy with the ancient process
of living, of dying.
                  We all have an instinct for expiring,
just as our bodies filter blood without a flinch
and the liver's ablution is as perfect
                         as the brook
that runs bloodstream-
                     like through the forest.
When the time comes, call off
        the endoscopes and probes:
                            let it be
like the theater of a thunderstorm,

             a wild conga dance up the spine,
or like the smart athleticism
of some kinds of silence.
All I know for sure
        is that I will be loaned out
                         to some other I.

T-Rex Stillborn

Stillborn, there's so much you haven't learned
and can't—what comets can do, for instance,
or a well-placed asteroid. Or even the what-ifs

of your existence: whether you could see in color
or bulk-eat five pounds a day during the heyday
of your growth spurt. Whether you could tear apart

the horn and frills of a triceratops in one bite
or two, and whether the perfume of its meat
on a humid night reeked more of Lizard God

or Egg Thief. What sights you missed: saber-tooth
birds and car-sized turtles, the sonic boom-
ing jaunts of sauropods, the inner sanctum

of your mother's skeleton. Imagine the foreplay,
the proto-feathers, the bone-shattering toe claws,
the domination of your species. I can; your downfall gave

me room. And when your ghost squirms
in my spleen, I know the foreboding's inbred.
What's a rex but a flash in the pan?

History of a Body

First it was the weight of a syllable,
a low hum of a being,
then a throb in the backcountry
of my body. I could feel the bits
piecing together: gill slits,
ear bones, fish tail, lower jaw.
I'm hitched to backache
& to this hard meridian bulge,
but they tell me I'm glowing.
The spur on the stem is intimating
fruit, growing like spider
veins weaving up & around
my calves. I know this:
the too-muchness of us
will be like scale built up inside a kettle.
What to do to do to do do do

Lycanthropy

the delusion that one has been turned into an animal,
particularly a wolf

I.   Analysis

It's not fiction or psychosis.
I lead parallel lives:
I work a nine to five,
knuckling down during the day,
then at the hour of vespers and neon
lights, padding across lawns and highways,
I return to the woods. When I breathe in
ice and pine needles, my flesh turns
to undercoat and ruffs of gray,
and myth hardens into real muscle, real bone-
crunching jaws. It begins as a prick
of the ears, a thrumming in my chest,
burrs strewn on matted fur, then I slip on
moonlight like a second coat, and take flight
across the vast bowl of night, sipping night air,
base notes of rabbit and rattlesnake musk
in my nose. Amber eye of terror
in the snakeweed, I arrive to claim what's mine.

II.   When We Go Hunting

The story's not just mine: at night
we are one, a pack, running down
the rabbits and white tail deer.
We know our place, in the back,
and we know the looks and smells
of reckoning: snout rooting around
the scrub, crush of tongue
in the wild rye. Luck's a wisp
of adrenalin caught in the underbrush.
We know the signs: antler-

scraped birches, half-moons
hoof-printed on the loosened dirt,
the smell of tender clover, smashed
and draggled through wet earth.
We hunt because the calling
sounds in our blood; you hunt to kill
time on the weekends. Doctor, unleash
your mind: can you hear with your notebook
in hand? My throat's open to you,
but try to pin me down, and you'll know
nothing of all the other names,
all the other lights and winds, silences
and scents, orders and omegas.
Only hounds and echoes at your door.

III.   Curative
                 —Testimonial by the Next of Kin, Fifty Years Later

"It is speculated that the rarity of the [lycanthropy] syndrome in Europe now is due
partly to the virtual extinction of wolves in Europe."
        —Stephen Juan, *The Odd Brain: Mysteries of Our Weird and Wonderful*
        Brains Explained

My grandmother no longer runs
with wolves. Most of them are gone,
killed off, and her fears have slackened too.
She's no longer musclebound, no longer
psychotic or dreamy-eyed at night.
Her worries, I'm glad to report,
are humdrum: like how to pay the rent,
how to stay busy when she's lonely.
Except once, riding on the highway
one moonlit night, she said she heard howls
from the mountain, and sucking the point
of her tooth, she claimed she smelled death.
She said there was blood on my hands.
I told her to relax, that the only wolves
were in her head.

Who Would Believe It

Superstition's credibility is shot again;
she courts misfortune more than not,
and implausible as she is, she sticks
around. You might see her at the sidewalk,
dropping her gloves or misbuttoning her coat,
then, flushing, twittering charms
into the cold air. But how can she trust herself?
She has no physical proof, no visible law
of being to live by, and to be beholden
to *what if* is half-curse, half-power.
What if fishing for clues in a closed
journal ends in wreckage? Or: *what if*
the impending smashup never comes
but keeps her in its thrall, in the way
of all worries that out-scale her size?
Or: *what if thinking can be treachery?*
                        So often Superstition
could not get the grime off her mind,
no matter how much she washed,
no matter if she knocked three times
or stayed up with moon on watch.
Rarely could she bask, snake-
like, in doubt, but had to nudge it, to tip
the balance in her favor. A body is nothing
but a long reckoning with dread,
but she believes the ravens,
back from some nesting errand,
would bring her a new nervous system,
auspicious as a crooked twig, and a mind
less like a nicked-up record player.
                        Still, even the atheist
blesses the sneezer.

But why? you press.
Why is shame to Superstition;
she has no reason. She just reads the signs,
puts herself in alliance with a version of faith
she only half-believes in, but needs
to ward off the dangerous limbo
of unknowing. What are the odds that love,
so given to smashups,

             will take off her coat

                     and stay awhile?

Octopus Dream

Every arm is a question,
a mind of its own;
the eighth, as if deliquescing,
slips through the keyhole
of my dreams, and the rest of her,
the sprawl and spread of her,
follows in tow. A cinch, she says,
slipping in between the cracks
of each world. Her clasp's tender,
and her suckers mouth my fingers, asking,
Why not, the base note of every dream.
Like shedding snakeskin,
I sling off my bones and join her,
our puddle-antics drawing stares.
Freaks, say the chancellors
of my subconscious (always the locker
room girls from high school, alien
to me in their newfound desires).
The shower drain spews vapor
like caldera, the air's close with steam,
and we—alternating moods like scarves—
blaze scarlet then slick ruby. And why not?
Unspooling, our arms go questing back
into that makeshift den
of memory where every glinting
hidden thing could be a vampire
fish or master lock,
its impossible combinations
irresistible, irresistible as the tides.

Next Those Antiques Will Be Missing

After Elizabeth Bishop's "Casabianca" and *Grey Gardens*

Memory's the big shabby house
edged out of the village, trying to hold
on when the present intrudes. Today Memory's
        surface tension. Tomorrow Memory
        will raid the cupboards, portraits for clues.

Memory's the squabbling women,
the dancing women, the creatures that skitter
in walls and corners. Dust stirs, and all's mayhem
        or wonder. And memory's root-
        ing out the keepsakes with the clutter.

Memory's the hinterland between song
and contention, that ancient argument
between mother and daughter
        about solicitude and sacrifice,
        and dreams like crenellated towers.

And Memory's lost again in overgrowth
or losing herself in a private march.
Memory's the stage, the prison, the call
        of sea salt in the air. And memory's
        raiding or rearranging each room.

Memories of Myself as a Galapagos Marine Iguana

I can almost remember my claws,
                        incurved like an eagle's,
my dorsal scales and tail
                    like a lash, my prehistoric body
                            outfitted like medieval weaponry.
I didn't have a name then for myself
                        or for the choke of boulders where I sunned.
I didn't have a name then for sun:
                    susurration of warmth at dawn
                        that grew louder each hour
until—by the thrumming
                of my blood—
I felt the sun's call in my muscles,
                in my re-activated heart.
                    Each noon, pulsating fire,
my body a darkening leather
                (as practical a conductor as copper),
I set out past the tuff, sword-sharp,
                and plunged off the cliff's edge
                        to return through an invisible door
back to the sea.
                I didn't have a name then for sea:
thraw of wave and cutting chill
                or for the hunger that urged me on
                        to seafloors carpeted with algae.
I grazed with fervor
                then in anguish if I lingered
too long in the cold.
                    I can almost remember the return:
                        back past the waves tossing ice
splinters into my back,
                    and past the sharks that prowled
counterclockwise above, and back to scale
                the sheer edge of the island.

I can go back and back and back,
and each time I pass through the thinnest thread
of a spider's web; it is the twitch you trace
for an instant on my face.
You doubt me?
This is not dreamed up.
This is the glossary at the end of your first primer.

Extinction Song

The animals went in two by two
but the endling went out alone.
The onliest of her breed,
she lived among the tinsel trees,

the twilled and rusting bars, the faux
orchids, the wards of last resorts.
The animals in threes went in,
but the endling went out alone,

although her heart she gave
to concrete, a statue the zoo
had made to look like her. Inside
of her was the heart and marrow

of earth and sun, and though she tried
and tried to make love to concrete,
no touch or warble was returned.
The animals went in four by four,

but the endling went out alone,
No ark to save her, no waiting wings,
no reckoning or second day.
Nothing left on earth to love or fear.

Leftovers

In Memory of Mike

I have un-marbled your lunch pail
of its jelly and mold sheen.
What to do now but finger the clasp, locked like a jaw?

Soon you'll exist as half relic,
half invention; we'll keep you
in shoe boxes, albums, drawers: you'll have to be dug out.

Your fingers hang on as compacts
and gray incrustations, whorled
impressions on your mirror's reflectionless glass.

I thumb the unmiraculous
detritus of your life, things
tricked into tenderness, the caps that hold your head's shape.

All's qualified and blessed: plastics
and boxers, the dandruff pearled
on the dresser, the sweat line plumbed down the threadbare shirt.

The Estate Sale

The lady lived here all her life, we're told.
It shows. We come to pick at what is left:
the closet's brood of shoes, the bristling dog-
eared furs, and elephantine skirts as sheer
as moth wings. We'll go away with ashtrays
and baubles, hatboxed china, TV trays
we'll later sell on ebay. Spent or broke,
we'll find—in death's uneven prudence—room
for more: her wooden fruits and cloth tulips,
her shatterproof bric-a-brac. All will cope;
the next of kin will manage what they must:
the lady's unpaid bills and dirge, while we
preserve the leftovers. *Better to pass*
these on than pass them up, a senior says.
Above our heads, the squirrels go skulking up
and down the eaves; the fattening month is here.

Nocturne

Hung up like black crepe
commemorating the night's feast,
a throng of bats in single file, rump to rump,
doze the day away. When dusk falls
and night, upside down, becomes coercive
as a magnet, they stir, click, and split
from their perch in near unison.
They are all appetite,
milk teeth and crooked fingers circling us
in our dreamtime: spirits on the bridges,
in the walls, atop the eaves.
If—half-awake—you stroked
one's back, its little bones
might remind you of Grandmother's hand,
light and trembling in yours,
a squeeze away from breaking.
Some loves are like that:
pervasive, ravenous in their hour,
but clutch too hard, and they will shatter.

Notes Towards an Apology

I pluck a tomato, dimpled
and over-ripe, size of an amputated heart.
Sun-scalded, it nearly pulses from the inside
out, the pulp bleeding from the skin
where my fingernails slit into it.
To rend: this is what I want.
And, more distantly, to make up, start again,
but instead I wed fury,
snatch her dowry of strop and switch-
blade and pelt the soggy tomato meat
of shame at the theater of our anger,
my throat lined with razors.
What came first: the fruit or the ache
to injure? And why does it live on
in my gut, toxic, if love
first set it there?

The Crocodiles He Keeps

Dad keeps crocodiles in our basement.
He's a collector of big reptiles: pythons with bite,
anacondas from Paraguay, the fittest Gilas,
even a Komodo once. He loves them all,
but crocs are his choice killers. Pleased even
by their bellows—mostly snorts and low gurgles by day,
grunts with a snorkel timbre by night—
he plays long B flats on his double bassoon
to get them sounding when Ma is away.
Vexed by bacteria and effluvia of croc chaw,
she tells Dad she's tired of their tails whipping her shins
every time she missteps on her way to wash laundry.
When her knitting circle visits,
she invents reasons to sit on the back deck
and blames the braying inside on the radiator
or the plumbing. "Sounds like fog horns,"
Mrs. O'Leary offers. Ma complains,
but explains she "won't defile" her husband's dream.
I'm twelve and I've lived the life span of four chameleons:
I know how to toss a herring into a caiman's waiting mouth,
how to squeeze the soil from a worm
so it won't catch in a hatchling's insides
when she feeds for the first time,
how to scrape the muck from a basement
creeping with snapping turtles without getting bitten.
And I know all about love, its tooth marks and cages,
its weird integrities.

The Mountaineer's Daughter

returned to the woods to be unmade.
               Her father went for the summit;
she for the traversal across
                    the forest floor, and all that came with it:
the quartz-flecked trail,
                   the soft belly
of the stream slurping under her feet,
           the grooves impressed on boulders
where glaciers screeched out
              a record of their passing.
She went to find prehistoric gneiss
        and ferns, still steadfast after all these years,
and all the things of the earth
      that are knitted into the grammar of time.
And she went to feel her humanness annihilated,
                 even if for awhile.

In the early owl-light, she searched for the source
         of the stream; she followed its amphibian undersong,
until night fell and—
      humming and waterlogged—
                   she found it.

Inside, she sensed her own time-
      table recording itself on her bones, and hoped
that someday another wanderer would find
      the curve of her spine,
          her long arms and splayed fingers,
             her worn gimbal joints at the hips,
       and know how far she journeyed to find herself

crouching at the cutbank
                with a colony of frogs,
called back by the centripetal pull of an early memory
          of belly flopping in,
                hindlimbs fully extended.

Wasp Nest

I hear them in my dreams;
their wings beat at a frequency of C,
and out of spittle, wood, and song,
they make a cathedral of paper mâché.
It grows each hour, a gothic fruit
below the sweet birch
while they writhe in a fever of toil,
laying comb upon comb,
feeding their larvae, fine-tuning their hive,
sounding their paean to female industry
through the streets. When I approach—
no, intrude—it is not pain that I crave,
but something close to it: her,
the queen of meticulous care
and fierce motherhood, whose madness
is formalized and made into a fortress.
I would be a pincushion to her stinger,
but instead she clutches me
as in a Klimt. Six little claws,
six little legs. Pillars of wasps rise
and fall away like gates when she comes.
And when she coaxes me through,
I will become her initiate,
just as someday a hive of sleepers
will pupate and rise from their combs,
such formal cells, to form a new brood.
There is venom here—
I cannot forget it, but nothing reckless.
There is pattern and her vision,
and life, a future, in every nurtured crevice.

Note

"The Crocodiles He Keeps" was inspired by Diane Ackerman's account of George, an alligator aficionado who did in fact keep crocodiles in his basement. In *The Moon by Whale Light*, Ackerman describes an occasion when George's pet alligators bellowed loudly from the depths of his basement on a day when his wife happened to have met with her sewing group.

Acknowledgments

I would like to thank Diane Goettel for believing in and making possible the publication of *The Death Spiral*. Thank you so much to my brilliant friends, many of whom were first readers for these poems, including Virginia Konchan, Amy Savage, Heather Treseler, jil hanifan, Therese Broderick, and Julie Guttman. A huge debt of gratitude to Charlotte Pence and April Ossmann for their invaluable advice and feedback on my manuscript.

And thank you to the following journals and anthologies, in which these poems first appeared (sometimes in different forms):

The Baltimore Review: "Family History"

Barzakh: "The Estate Sale"

Tupelo Quarterly: "Leftovers"

Flyway: "The Crocodiles He Keeps" and "Wasp Nest"

The Fourth River: "Newtok, Alaska"

Ecotone: "The Mountaineer's Daughter" and "The Second Moon Colony Will Not Fail"

Denver Quarterly: "Memories of Myself as a Galapagos Marine Iguana"

Nimrod: "Nocturne" and "Eighty Beats"

Permafrost: "Bearings" and "History of a Body"

Terrain: "Thirst in the Chihuahuan Desert," "Night Shift," and "Prognosis: Releasable"

Pittsburgh Poetry Review: "Mammoth Resurrected" and "Secrets of the Magician's Assistant"

Sundress Publication's "Best of the Net" 2016 Anthology: "Family History"

Not My President Anthology (Thoughtcrime Press): "Wishes for Emily in the Age of Trump"

Cosmonauts Avenue: "Terlingua, TX Haibun"

Grist: "River Road"

Revisiting the Elegy in the Black Lives Matter Era (Routledge): "Nina"

Matter: "Slave Patrols and Night Watches" and "America: Revenge Poem #4"

Tin House: "The Fourth Anniversary"

Permissions

Excerpts from the following publications have been used with permission:

The Odd Brain © 2006 by Dr. Stephen Juan. Published by Andrews McMeel Publishing.

"For Amorous Bald Eagles, a 'Death Spiral' Is a Hot Time" © July 2016 by Patricia Edmonds. Published by *National Geographic*.

Sarah Giragosian is the author of the poetry collection *Queer Fish*, a winner of the American Poetry Journal Book Prize (Dream Horse Press, 2017) and *The Death Spiral*. The craft anthology, *Marbles on the Floor: How to Assemble a Book of Poems*, which is co-edited by Sarah and Virginia Konchan, is forthcoming from The University of Akron Press. Sarah's poems and non-fiction essays have appeared in such journals as *Ecotone, Tin House, Prairie Schooner, Orion,* and *The Missouri Review,* among others. She teaches at the University at Albany-SUNY.